Hey!

You Aren't the Boss of Me!

by

Bob Fessler

INKWATER
PRESS

PORTLAND • OREGON
INKWATERPRESS.COM

www.inkwaterpress.com

ISBN-13 978-1-59299-262-1
ISBN-10 1-59299-262-5

Publisher: Inkwater Press

Printed in the U.S.A.

This book is dedicated to my six grandchildren who bring me joy and inspiration. Kyle, Kaitlyn, Jayden, Vandon, Autumn and Maddox are my heroes. I thank my high school sweetheart, love of my life, and beautiful wife, Susan, for all of her love and support. It is her belief in me that gives me the confidence to write.

© The Picture People

HEY! REMEMBER, YOU AREN'T THE BOSS OF ME!

Bob Fersch

Part

1

Hey, You Aren't the Boss of Me

I've tried to wish, I've tried to pray
But nothing works; I've got to say
No matter what I try to do,
My sister just keeps coming through

She comes into my room at night
She enters in the broad daylight
I tell her no, I say to stay
But she just comes in anyway

She takes my stuff when I say no
She even took my G. I. Joe
When I say stop, she says to me
"Hey, you aren't the boss of me"

She took the ball I like to throw
She took the plant I was trying to grow
She grabbed my comb, she grabbed my glove
She grabbed the football that I love

A top, some pop, a licorice stick
The soccer ball I love to kick
A candy bar, a jar, potato chips
She even took my plastic lips

She took my globe, my kicking tee
And then she screams, "You aren't the boss of me"
My bubble gum, my cushioned chair
Pens and pencils, . . .my underwear

She took my lamp, she took the shade
She'll take it all, I am afraid
I hear her coming down the hall
To swipe the mirror from my wall

My baseball cards, my DVD's
My ribbons from my spelling bees
"I'll tell Mom, you wait and see"
She just says, "You aren't the boss of me"

My shoes, my pillow, my Dr. Suess
I could tie it down, but she'll knock it loose
My program from the Yankee game
A coloring book, a picture frame

My full size poster of Britney Spears
My bike that has at least ten gears
My jar that has a big green frog
She even took a Lincoln log

Some coins, a shirt, a pair of dice
A super shot of Jerry Rice
I know my sister's only three
But she still says, "You aren't the boss of me"

And now my mom just broke the news
I thought I had no more to lose
As if my life could be more wild
She's going to have another child

Mom sat me down and said, "Hey, mister,
You're going to have another sister"
Lock my door and hide the key
Two girls to say, "You aren't the boss of me"

Skully the Skunk

Skully the Skunk was a black and white hunk
He had everything going except that he stunk
He was studly and handsome and really looked great
But the stink really stunk, it was stink you would hate

Skully would come out at night, he'd come out quite late
This hunk of a skunk, you would think he could date
His beautiful smile would make the girls swoon
But the odor was so bad, they'd stay inside till noon

This made Skully quite sad cuz he wanted to date
He wanted a girlfriend, he just wanted a mate
But the smell just got worse the older he got
The stench was too awful even though he was hot

He was anxious to date so he asked out a cat
Then a dog, then a pig, then an ugly old bat
But they all told him "NO!" They said that he stunk
He was sad, he felt bad; poor old Skully the Skunk

So what could he do to get rid of the stink?
He crawled into his hole so he could quietly think
He'd find him some water. He'd swim in the lake
That would get rid of the stink. That is all it would take

So he washed and he bathed as he dipped in the lake
Then he climbed onto shore and he dried with a shake
He then took a deep breath and inhaled through his nose
To find that his stench did not smell like a rose

Then he found himself an old aerosol can
That he sprayed and he sprayed. This would be a good plan
But wouldn't you know, the smell was still strong
The stink mixed with sweet really smelled very wrong

But then it all happened on the sunniest day
A skunk we'll call Sally with a horrible spray
She was pretty and black with a really white stripe
And an odor so nasty, she was really quite ripe

But Skully thought that she smelled like perfume
With her big bushy tail that looked like a plume
She was gorgeous and snappy and really quite fine
So he asked her inside and asked her to dine

So Skully had found the love of his life
This black and white critter was now Skully's wife
They waddled off to live near Sonoma
While thoroughly enjoying each other's aroma

Freddy the Frog

A long time ago in a land far away
In the month of September, no .. no, I think it was May
Deep in this swamp in a very dark bog
Lived Freddy the Frog inside of this log

Freddy was different than most other frogs
He could squeal like the hogs and bark like the dogs
He could speak like a human in English or Greek
But because of these traits others called him a geek

He could make lots of noises, but he just couldn't croak
So his friends laughed at him and called him a joke
This made him sad, so he stayed in his log
Deep in this swamp in this very dark bog

Then on the 13th of May, no, it was the 19th of June
Freddy awakened to an unusual tune
He looked out the window of his humble abode
To find singing outside this rather strange looking toad

This toad had warts all over its face
Not only the face, but all over the place
The toad was wearing a bright yellow thong
With warts and a thong, this just had to be wrong

So he yapped like a terrier and squealed like the pigs
That was just Freddy's way of sharing his digs
He was trying to be nice, but the toad looked so weird
The toad wasn't just ugly, it was growing a beard

"What's your name?" Freddy asked to this toad with a thong
"I'm Natashia." Said the toad to the tune of a song
"You're a girl?" Freddy noted as he gasped for his breath
A girl with this face nearly scared him to death

But Natashia explained that she wasn't a toad
She was turned to a toad at her humble abode
She was really a princess who was changed by a spell
Changed by a wizard with some gel and a yell

You can help me return if you give me a kiss
A kiss on the mouth and be sure you don't miss
You'll make me a princess and help me get back
If you'll give me your frog lips and give me a smack

So Freddy obliged and gave Natashia his lips
He gave her a kiss and began doing flips
And when he awoke after feeling a poke
There stood the toad, but . . Freddy could croak

She wasn't a princess and still was a toad
With warts and the thong eating pie ala-mode
"What just happened?" asked Freddy as he croaked out this noise
Freddy's ribbett, it sounded like the rest of the boys

"I'm not who I said, I'm not who you think."
Said this toad with the warts and a thong that turned pink
Then the toad ate a fly and croaked through her gizzard
"I'm not really a toad, I'm really the wizard."

I hated the fact that you hated your voice
Now your friends won't mock you when you let out a noise
Then Natashia slid back off the log to the bog
And left Freddy behind as a ribbetting frog

So be careful when driving along in your car
When your headlights are shining, but not very far
When something is hopping and crossing the road
It might be the wizard dressed up as a toad

The Gator with the Cloak and the Cup

Mom said "Bye" and closed the front door
She said she was heading out to the store
When she left she smiled and waved back at me
She said you be good, I'll be back home by three

After she left, just a few minutes later
I looked out the window and saw a green gator
The gator was walking and standing straight up
He was wearing a cloak and carrying a cup

He walked to my window and looked back at me
And said that he knew Mom would be home by three
So he said let me in, through the house we can run
You can let me in now; we could really have fun

I knew that I shouldn't. Mom would really be mad
I knew that I shouldn't. This could really be bad
But the gator came in with his cup and his cloak
He made me giggle when he told me a joke

Then he opened the door and you'll never believe
In came a hippo and a rhino named Steve
Then a lynx with some drinks and a seal with some meals
An ape with a cape who was wearing high heels

A monkey named Fred came in like a shot
Then an elephant entered with a pan and a pot
A bear with some hair came in with a ham
Then a bat with a hat brought some bread and some jam

Then a gorilla walked by with some cake and a steak
I looked at the steak and it didn't look fake
These birds said some words when they flew into my house
One was a robin and one was a grouse

This giraffe with this neck that could reach to the sky
And an huge elephant who said he could fly
They squeezed through the door and sat on my couch
Then in hopped a kangaroo with a kid in her pouch

My house was so full and it looked like a zoo
With this many animals it smelled like one too
They were making a mess, they were spilling their food
They were lewd, they were crude, they were really quite rude

Then they left all this mess at a quarter till three
Food on the floor, what a mess left to see
Mom will be home at three, as she said
When Mom sees this mess I will really be dead

When she entered the house and she saw with her eyes
This mess and the trash that was covered with flies
She dropped all her things as she saw all this mess
She said how'd this happen, you better confess

I said, "Okay, Mom. I can really explain"
It happened like this, but you'll think I'm insane
She didn't believe me so I went to my room
I sat in a corner with some doom and some gloom

I was to be grounded at least for a week
She wouldn't believe me, this all seemed so bleak
Then all of a sudden, Mom let out a shout
I ran to her side to see what that was about

When she opened the curtains and looked through the crack
The gator with the cup and the cloak looked right back
And standing beside him; just standing right there
Was the ape with the cape and the bear with the hair

So the moral of the story and the lesson to you
If you return to your house and it smells like a zoo
It wasn't your children that messed everything up
It was likely the gator with the cloak and the cup

Haircut

This is the story of young Billy Smith
This story is real. It isn't a myth
Billy had freckles and hair that was red
A dalmatian named Speckles and a brother named Ned

But his hair that was red was getting too long
He needed a haircut. Not to get it was wrong
He needed to go to the barber for sure
His hair got so long it was looking like fur

His hair grew longer with each passing day
Get my haircut today? I think not! No way!
I won't let them clip it. I won't let them cut
I'll just hide under my bed and keep my door shut

So his hair started growing. It grew past his neck
It would catch on the chairs when he'd play on the deck
It grew down his back. It grew down to his waist
Just letting it grow just seemed in poor taste

His hair got so long it went to his knees
It got dirty and sticky and I think he had fleas
It got longer and longer as it grew and it grew
His hair was still red as it grew to his shoes

His hair got so long that it dragged on the ground
It was droopy and goopy and bugs could be found
He had things living in there that you wouldn't believe
He had critters in there that you wouldn't retrieve

So time kept on passing at least for a year
This story is true, at least that's what I hear
This is going to sound awful, I think it's a shock
His hair got so long that it circled the block

There's no way he could wash it, not even with rain
And to wash it inside would just clog up the drain
Now more creatures were found on the top of his head
Some that were living and some that were dead

His hair got so sticky and covered with dirt
And when cars would run over it, you'd think it would hurt
Now everyone wished he would just cut his hair
His hair got so filthy, it was polluting the air

You've got to believe me as weird as this sounds
His hair got so long, it weighed 4,000 pounds
His hair got so heavy that he had to lay still
And what happens next just gives me a chill

His hair crossed the county and then crossed the state
Then what happened next could only be fate
It caught on a train and it dragged him away
And young Billy Smith hasn't been seen since that day

He just needed a haircut, as simple as that
Fur only belongs on your dog or your cat
Don't let your hair grow. Don't let it be long
To let it get long would be dangerously wrong

So when Mom says it's time to go to the shop
Don't slow down or stop if your hair looks like a mop
If Mom says, "It's time. It's time for haircuts."
Don't even think twice. No ifs, ands or buts!

Mickey the Monkey

Mickey the Monkey was a little bit funky
He hated the fact he was a little bit chunky
But he couldn't resist to eat a banana
He'd eat in the shade underneath his cabana

He'd eat and he'd eat, he would munch on a bunch
Bananas were great for breakfast or lunch
So Mickey the Monkey, the funky but chunky
Was really becoming more and more clunky

He loved to dance and show he could move
But as he kept gaining girth he was losing his groove
He was starting to develop a big baboon hiney
It was getting quite red and getting quite shiney

A rhesus and gibbon, gorilla and chimp
All laughed at Mickey and called him a blimp
So Mickey the funky, the chunkiest monkey
Was a banana junkie who wasn't so spunky

So what should we say to Mickey the Monkey
To help him feel better and not feel so gunky?
Tell Mickey the chunky, who lives in Savannahs
Say Mickey, STOP EATING SO MANY BANANAS!!

I Wouldn't Want to Be a Mom

Clean the dishes in the sink
Mom, I could really use a drink
Thanks for cooking me a waffle
To be a mom would be quite awful

Wash the laundry, fold it up
Clean up dog mess from the pup
Drive me to a baseball game
To be a mom would be a shame

Pick up clothing off the floor
Put the Band-Aid on the sore
Cook up dinner for my dad
To me a mom would be quite sad

Comb my hair when I awake
Clean the tub, for goodness sake
Scream at me for my bad grades
Clean the dust from window shades

Make the beds when all are gone
Call the doctor on the phone
Take out garbage once a week
Find us playing hide and seek

Wipe the boogers from my nose
Clean the goop between my toes
Run the water for my bath
Help me when I do my math

Yell at me when I am bad
Calm me down when I am mad
Take me to a movie show
Sit with me on the front row

Watch her soaps each day at noon
Take me out to see the moon
Vacuum floors to clear the dust
Make a pie with homemade crust

Clean the litter for the cat
Why would anyone do that
I'd hate to be a mom, I think
To be a mom would really stink

What could make this worth the fuss
To raise a couple of kids like us
I guess my mom just might be crazy
One thing's for sure, she isn't lazy

I asked my mom why she does this
On my forehead she laid a kiss
She sat me down upon the chair
And rubbed her fingers on my hair

She took her eyes and looked in mine
Her smile made me feel so fine
She said she does it all, you see
She does everything to be with me

My Favorite Holiday

January, February, March, April, May
Which day of the year is the best holiday
There's Christmas and Easter, the Fourth of July
I must pick out my favorite, I'll give it a try

My teacher said pick one and tell it to me
That's a really hard question, which one would it be
No matter how hard I think with my brain
To pick out just one seems really insane

There's Halloween, New Years and Valentine's Day
Which one is my favorite, that's so hard to say
I love getting presents when Santa Claus comes
Maybe this year, he'll bring me my drums

The Easter Bunny hops through my yard with his legs
And covers the grass with bright easter eggs
My girlfriend at school gave me a red valentine
That said, when I opened it, "Would you be mine?"

Why would my teacher do this to me?
Pick out just one? I'd rather pick three
Even three's not enough. I need to pick eight
If I could pick all, that would really be great

In fact if I could, I'd create even more
I'd add days to the list, more than ever before
June has no holiday, it really needs one
The last day of school seems to really be fun

There's Mother's Day; Father's Day; each has their own
A day for my dog? We could throw him a bone
We could have a holiday to celebrate Clem
Or a day for my friends, Timmy and Jim

My birthday it comes only one time a year
It's not even close, I wish it was near
I'd like to have birthdays at least once a week
We could play lots of games, we could play hide and seek

My friends could come over and eat lots of cake
Add 52 birthdays, that's all it would take
Fill boxes with presents and give them to me
Pack them and stack them as high as a tree

Fill my bedroom, the closet, my sister's room too
If I had all those presents, then what would I do?
I know what I'd do, it will help with my grade
This is such a good thought, there will be a parade

I'll load up a semi and drive to the school
A semi at school would break every rule
But my teacher will enjoy this, she'll be happy for sure
When she finds that the presents were given to her

The Game

The stadium filled with anticipation
The weatherman promised no precipitation
There was electricity in the air
Fans had come from everywhere

The word had really traveled round
Superstar Kyle Wilson had come to town
He'd wear his famous "25"
Thousands came to see him live

The TV cameras were warming up
Coca Colas in the cup
Fans wearing the home team's hat
Excited to see Kyle Wilson bat

The game went on, the game stayed tied
There was no score on either side
Inning six, then seven, then eight
As tensions climbed, the noise was great

The game was tied at the end of nine
The championship was on the line
When their man came up to hit
The catcher lifted up his mitt

The pitcher threw a fastball by
The anxious crowd let out a sigh
The next pitch went beside Kyle's head
The crowd went silent, the place was dead

The next ball curved across the plate
He swung quite hard, he couldn't wait
The umpire raised his arm, strike two
Kyle tapped the bat against his shoe

The pitcher stood upon the mound
He picked some dirt up from the ground
He looked and took the catcher's signs
Kyle stood tall between the lines

The pitcher began to wind again
The fans were pounding on the tin
The lightning pitch began to sing
And Slugger Kyle began to swing

The crowd stood up when Kyle connected
Toward the fence, the ball directed
Their superstar had won the game
Kyle Wilson added to his fame

He tipped his hat toward the crowd
The screaming fans became quite loud
Kyle was now the MVP
He did it for the world to see

Then suddenly a voice yelled out
Kyle whirled his head and looked about
The sound he heard could be no other
The voice was clearly from his mother

Dinnertime she called to Kyle
He dropped his bat for a little while
He'd go inside and eat some food
This interruption had killed the mood

But when he was done he'd return to play
The crowd would come back anyway
Kyle began to feel much better
After all, this was a doubleheader

The Dilemma

It's Saturday, my chores are through
Doing chores just makes me blue
But now that I am rid of them
I think I'll go outside with Clem

Clem is my friend down the street
To play with him is quite a treat
He likes to throw the ball to me
He likes to climb up in the tree

He likes to look for colored stones
He likes to give me ice cream cones
We like to run along with Mac
We like to run around the track

Mac the dog is Clem's brown schnauzer
Who likes to pull and yank my trouser
But Clem's not home so that is out
I wonder why. What's that about?

It's Saturday, my chores are through
And Clem is gone. Now what to do?
Mom might take me to the store
Now that would really be a bore

I could help Dad mow the lawn
That would really make me yawn
I could dig a hole out back
I could put it in a sack

I could play upon my swing
I could pick a song to sing
I could watch a cartoon show
I could play with my big toe

I could sit outside with Sis
That's a joy I'll try to miss
I could stand upon my head
I could hide beneath my bed

I could grab some cards to deal
I could watch my sunburn peel
I could eat a candy bar
I could catch bugs in a jar

I could play some pick up sticks
With Clem not home I'm in a fix
I could play with Lincoln Logs
I could catch some big green frogs

I could catch a snail to eat
Now that would really be a treat
Catch a butterfly or caterpillar
Play with Dad's roto-tiller

It sure is quiet, don't you see
And I am bored as I can be
I could clean wax from my ear
I sure do hate that Clem's not here

What's that noise. A car went by.
I'll go outside for one more try
It's Clem! It's Clem! He's really in
To play with Clem would make me grin

What's that he says, he can't play now
If he can't play, I'll have a cow
He screamed to me outside his doors
I have to go in and do my chores

The Name Game

I'm going to have a new sister or brother
I learned this from my pregnant mother
She said I have a job to do
Name the baby, it's up to you

She said she'd leave it up to me
Pick a name from A to Z
I thought and thought about this job
I thought so hard my head did throb

This must be an important task
Otherwise, why would she ask?
Brandy, Sandy, Randy, Andy
Maybe we could name it Mandy

Jill and Phil and Bill and Will
This is hard, but it's a thrill
Lynn and Glen and Ben and Jen
Sammy, Pammy, Cammy, Tammy

Sue and Lew and Stu and Drew
Oh, I wish this job was through
Ike and Mike, Jack and Mac
I think I'm having a heart attack

Harry, Mary, Kerrie, Jerry
Larry, Perry, . . . Halle Berry
Freddy, Teddy, Lori and Tori
Oh, this job is making me sorry

I wonder if it's a boy or a girl
If it's a girl, I'll name it Pearl
Maybe I would name her Jan
Or better yet, I'll name her Anne

If it's a boy, that could be rough
Boys' names are kind of tough
Maybe I would name him Billy
All this thinking is making me silly

Instead of Van or Dan
I'll name him . . . Peter Pan
I know, I think I'll name him Shrek
Or Superman, what the heck

As I ponder on the couch
How about this name? Oscar the Grouch
The more I think, the more I'm tryin'
I think I'll name him the Cowardly Lion

I wonder if Mom would think it's best
If I name her the Wicked Witch of the West
Barney's good or G. I. Joe
Larry, Curly, or even Moe

I better hurry and shake a legga
I think I'll call it Rutabaga
Oh, Oh, here comes Mom to check on me
This list of names she cannot see

Hi, Mom. I think I figured out the name
I think I really like this game
If it's a boy, I'll name it Kyle
I thought about it for quite a while

If it's a girl, I think you'll see
That Kaitlyn is the name for me
Then Mom left. Whew! That was close
I actually think this game is gross

What Could I Do?

If I could make a difference and help the world improve
If I could choose just one good thing to help things really move
What would I do to make things right and make bad go away?
What could I do to make things bright and make life a sunny day?

I'd like to feed the hungry and give them all some food
If I could help them all be full, that would help improve the mood
If I could help those who are so poor to have more than they do
I'd give them all some money, so they could buy things too

If I could give the world some peace so all could get along
If I could make everything right, and no one did things wrong
If I could heal the tired and sick, and help them all get well
I'd like to help those who are down and help up those who fell

I'd like to help the kids on drugs, or kids who go and steal
If I could make them understand how other people feel
I'd like to help the handicapped. I'd help those who are impaired
I'd make them walk without their pain with everything repaired

I'd like for everyone who died to make their way to heaven
I'd like to do all of these things, if only I weren't seven
I know what's right, but I'm too small to really do a thing
But if I pray and ask the Lord, he'll make the angels sing

I think if everyone stopped and prayed and asked for God to aid
That with his help, if we would ask, the bad would start to fade
I wonder why adults I see just go on with their day
When they see the sun behind the clouds and skies have turned to gray

Find the Missing President

Let's play a game that is just for fun
See if you can figure out the missing one
We've had 43 presidents, White House residents
Which one is missing from the following evidence?

Washington, Jefferson, Madison, Jackson
Pay close attention with no distraction
Nixon, Fillmore, Roosevelt, Ford
If you don't get this, you're out of your gourd

Coolidge, Arthur, Carter and Lincoln
If you can't get this, you're really stinkin'
Cleveland and Cleveland, Bush and Bush
You can do it. Push! Push! Push!

Johnson and Johnson, Clinton and Polk
Please don't miss this, please don't choke
Roosevelt, Reagan, Truman and Hoover
If you get this, you're a shaker and mover

Harding, Hayes, Taft, Eisenhower
Keep on trying. You've got the power
Adams, Adams, Monroe and Pierce
Pull this off and you're really fierce

Harrison, Harrison, Tyler, Taylor
This would be simple for a drunkin' sailor
Garfield, Kennedy, Van Buren and Grant
Can you do it? I bet you can't

McKinley, Buchanan, that's 42
Getting the last is up to you
There's one that's missing. Please don't pout
Now get to work and figure it out

Me

I never stumble and never fumble
I'm usually sweet and always humble
The thousands of people that I see
Never look quite as good as me

I dress the best and have huge guns
I know the girls must love my buns
They must wish they could kiss my lips
Or just stand back and observe my hips

My chest is large. I'm really buff
I hate to brag about my stuff
But all the guys wish they could be
Handsome devils just like me

The girls love my face and love my dimples
It is so smooth and has no pimples
My teeth are perfect and pearly white
My wavy hair is out of sight

My smile is warm and turns girls on
My personality is really fun
The players want me in their huddle
The babes all wish that they could cuddle

I keep a picture on my shelf
A color photo of myself
To remind me that I long to be
Not like you and just like me

So I must go. I have a date
I must be prompt and not be late
The two of us have a real connection
I have a date with my reflection

But I Don't Want to Go to Bed!!

"I'm scared." Jayden sheepishly said
Right after Mom placed her softly in bed
No more excuses, honey. You've run out of time
Would you please go to sleep if I read you a rhyme?

Yes, read me a rhyme, said Jayden to her mommy
Then afterwards said, "I have an ache in my tummy"
I'm thirsty, Mom, could you get me a drink?
I think I can sleep with a drink from the sink

Would you open my door? My room is too dark
When I wake up tomorrow can we play in the park?
I have a big boo-boo right there on my knee
Could I have a band-aid? Please get one for me

I can't find my doll. Could you find it for me?
Oh, Oh, you won't like this, but I have to go pee
My blanket is twisted and doesn't feel right
I'm scared of the dark. Could you turn on a light?

It's hot in my room. Could you turn on the fan?
Oh no, my pillow's outside in the van
Could I have a cookie and then go to sleep?
If you give me a cookie, you won't hear a peep

Now I am cold. Could you turn off the fan?
I have to go poop. May I go to the can?
Please look in my closet. I heard a strange noise
May I get up from my bed and play with my toys?

Do you care if the dog goes to sleep on my bed?
Now the dog has its butt way too close to my head
Could you make the dog move? He's beginning to snore
Please make him leave and stay outside the door

Then Mom lost all color inside of her face
Her sweetness was leaving. It was leaving this place
Her veins started popping on the front of her head
It certainly appeared that I was about to be dead

I think that I played this as long as I could
If I faked one more story, it wouldn't be good
I set a new record for staying awake
And never even needed the one on the snake

When I Grow Up

When I grow up, I want to be
Something special, you wait and see
When I'm all grown, when I am through
What will I be, what will I do?

Maybe I can put out fires
Maybe I can change the tires
Maybe I can fix a car
Maybe I could play guitar

I might like to sell some shoes
Or play piano and sing the blues
Work with dogs and be a vet
I could cure your ailing pet

I might like to be an actor
Or learn to be a chiropractor
Football is my favorite game
I'll be great, they'll know my name

I could grow up to be a teacher
Or maybe I could be a preacher
If I'm a doctor, I'll cure cancer
I'll come up with every answer

I could host a TV show
I'd show the world how much I know
Maybe I could be a cop
Say when to go and when to stop

When I grow up I'll be the boss
Or be a coach without a loss
I could end up President
And be a White House resident

I might like biology
Psychology or Geology
Accounting might be what I do
When I am grown, when I am through

All these sound so really cool
Almost all require school
I could end up one of these
If I just make all A's and B's

But I know what would please me most
Something that would make me boast
To be like him would not be bad
I'd like to be just like my Dad

Directions?

Although we've been driving in circles for hours
Through back roads and side roads and fields of flowers
Through gravel, through snow, through highways of frost
Don't worry, don't sweat, don't think that I'm lost

I know where I am. . . . I don't need a map
Just sit over there. We'll be there in a snap
I'm a man of the world, a man of connections
I'll never, not ever, ask for directions

I know that you're mad and you want me to stop
You want to get there in order to shop
Quit looking at me. I don't need inspections
I won't stop. You won't pop. I'm not asking directions

I know where we are. I know where we're at
Stop nagging at me. Hold on to your hat
You'd think we were looking for some kind of grail
Not asking directions doesn't mean that I'm male

Quit hassling me. Quit smacking your lips
Just reach in the back and grab me the chips
It won't do you good to threaten rejections
I'm not pulling over and asking directions

I wish you were silent and falling asleep
I think that by talking, you're getting in deep
Complaining and yapping with constant inflections
Can't make me stop and ask for directions

Oh, no! Behind me is a cop with a light
I pulled off of the road; I pulled off to the right
He walked to my window. He walked with a flurry
He said, " Where are you going in such a big hurry?"

My wife started laughing. She thought that was cute
She chuckled and snickered and let out a hoot
So I thought rather quickly and after reflections
I said to the cop, "Could you give me directions?"

Autumn in the Spring

When the sky was blue and the grass was green
On the most beautiful day I've ever seen
While the sparrows chirped and the robins sing
God gave me Autumn in the spring

As the trees grew leaves and the flowers bloom
As the day grew bright and removed the gloom
On this perfect day I wouldn't change a thing
When God gave me Autumn in the spring

I never knew when I met my wife
How much this girl would change my life
My gift to her was just a ring
She gave to me Autumn in the spring

I thank the lord, my God above
For giving me two girls to love
My wife's my queen and I'm her king
And now my princess . . . Autumn in the spring

Domestic Airliner

Inspired by a True Story

It started out such a beautiful day
The world was right in every way
In Carolina nothing could be finer
Unless you're flying on a domestic airliner

My seat belt was fastened and we were leaving on time
The flight attendant gave her spiel with a rhyme
The passenger's faces all had a smile
But that wouldn't last, that would change in a while

The pilot announced that we've noticed a flaw
"On a tire we've noticed it's a little bit raw.
We'll change it now and it won't take too long."
He smiled and winked with a dance and a song

For hours we watched this little old man
Stare at the tire, this man had no plan
We boarded the flight just a little too late
To catch the connection at our connecting gate

Every flight in this country had been overbooked
If you missed your connection you would be overlooked
"I'm sorry to tell you there's no flights left today.
If you're willing to standby you can catch this in May."

"You can stay in a motel, we'll cover the cost
But I'm sorry to tell you, your bags have been lost.
And sir, we would like it if you'd not be a whiner.
Please just relax and enjoy our domestic airliner."

"I know that you want to get to the coast
But your holiday plans are most certainly toast.
If you'd like, we could send your wife pretty flowers
While you sit in this airport for hours and hours."

"There's a seat that's come open on the 7th of June,
But it's actually on the shuttle and it goes to the moon.
We could rent you a car if they weren't already taken.
Why sir, you don't look happy, you look rather shaken."

"We gave you a voucher to buy you some food,
So after three days why are you being so rude?
Your luggage was located and put on a jet.
Unfortunately, the jet is off for Tibet."

"Oh . . . you're wife has sent papers. She wants a divorce.
She left you the kids, but she's taking the Porsche.
We hope that you've found that this problem is minor.
We thank you for flying our domestic airliner."

The Most Beautiful Girl I'd Ever Seen

What was her name, what would it be?
I wonder if she'd dance with me
When I was young and just sixteen
The most beautiful girl I'd ever seen

I held her hand in mine that night
Her smile was sweet, it felt so right
She danced with me, we stepped and swayed
She smiled at me as the music played

I fell for her the night we met
It took her longer, much longer yet
It took a year when she was ready
I asked this girl if she'd go steady

I loved her face, I loved her smile
To be with her I'd walk a mile
She was always sweet and never mean
The most beautiful girl I'd ever seen

I must be blessed, as luck would be
She said that she would marry me
We fell more in love with every day
I loved this girl in every way

We had three kids and watched them grow
We showed them love, we let it show
It went so fast and now they're gone
It was so great, it was so fun

Yet after that, we're still in love
I thank the lord, thank God above
As the skies are blue and the trees are green
She's the most beautiful girl I'd ever seen

The grandkids are the greatest thing
We watch them play, we watch them sing
We still hold hands, I love her smile
We love to cuddle for a while

And then this day, she told me this
I knew that something was amiss
The doctor called her with an answer
It may be bad, it may be cancer

We waited weeks, we suffered so
Please don't leave me. Please don't go
I loved her since I was a teen
The most beautiful girl I'd ever seen

I waited in the waiting room
She was my bride, I was her groom
The surgeon opened up the door
He walked to me across the floor

My heart was racing in my chest
Awaiting if she passed the test
She was my girl, she was my dancer
The doctor said it wasn't cancer

She is my friend, she is my wife
But most of all, she is my life
And now I have another chance
To ask my wife if she would dance

She smiles at me and holds my hand
Another dance to another band
I've loved her since I was a teen
The most beautiful girl, I'd ever seen

Printed in the United States
91009LV00001BA

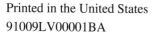